She's A 10

The Black Woman's Guide to Embracing Personal & Professional Greatness

Dr. Maria Shantell Williams

ISBN: 978-0-578-87839-3

Printed in the United States of America

Visit www.drmariashantell.com for free resources to help you on your journey of embracing personal and professional **greatness**!

CONTENTS

Always & Forever in My Heart

Alicia Danielle Peterson

Aug. 2, 1986- May 20, 2019

DEDICATION

To the most beautiful angel in heaven, my sweet sister, Alicia, who left us way too soon.

I have always admired your ability to dream outside of your comfort zone and your boldness in creating new business ideas.

Thank you for showing me and countless others what it looks like to live fearless, even during your last days on earth.

Since your passing on May 20, 2019, I have been encouraged to reach higher heights and put my foot on the gas like never before! The way you smiled and lived through good times, as well as moments of adversity, will always be cherished. I will continue to make sure your pride and joy, Kam, is good in your absence. You inspired so many of us by being such an amazing mother to him. You are forever and always in our hearts. See you on the other side.

FOREWORD

I have looked to the women in my life for inspiration for as long as I can remember. From my childhood in Chicago, my time in college, and throughout my adult life, I have been led and encouraged by strong Black women along the way.

We live in a world where immense pressure is placed on African American women. Yet, time and time again, we often step up to help those around us to ensure our collaborative success. The support from those around me has been especially important throughout my career in public service and has proven to be essential during my tenure as the first woman and first African American woman elected as Mayor-President of East Baton Rouge Parish.

This collective approach to success is essential to our success, but amongst the chaos we must recognize the importance of balance. Balancing your relationships, your work, your passions, and most importantly, finding balance within yourself. These lessons are sometimes learned the hard way, but they are essential for our prosperity; as the saying goes, "you can't pour from an empty cup."

Balance is achieved through prioritizing your wellness; this mindset is essential for your longevity, and it allows you to best contribute to those around you.

In this book, you will learn and understand how to embrace your strengths, assess your weaknesses, and channel them into the tools you need to achieve success. Our highs and lows are central to our development and wellness. They are what makes us unique and allow us to embrace greatness.

As you read, I encourage you to take the lessons from each chapter and apply them to your life. Using the lessons you will learn to assess your challenges, embrace your truth, and lay your foundation for success.

At times our journeys may be tough — it is important to remember these experiences are what make you, you. Reflect on your lived experience. Embrace the moment you are in. Learn from it and grow. These experiences can be channeled to progress your success and lead those around you into prosperity.

As Maria says in her book, "If you can overcome, you can overcome again." I hope you take these lessons and never stop overcoming as you work towards your successes.

Sharon Weston Broome
Mayor-President, City of Baton Rouge

INTRODUCTION

Welcome to another level of embracing Greatness! By the end of reading this book, you will be inspired to see your personal and professional obstacles as opportunities for growth, be equipped with practical tools and strategies, and receive the inspiration you need to boldly own *your* Greatness!

The average black woman struggles with making time for herself because she often attempts to be everything for everyone else around her. Additionally, many black women are raised believing they are Superwomen and accept the false notion that they must constantly juggle multiple tasks without dedicating time for themselves. While this usually results in the outward appearance of being okay, most women end up suffering internally in areas that are less visible to others. Furthermore, a great majority of black women shy away from communicating their needs due to pain from past disappointments or fear that they will be negatively judged by others. The end result is usually burnout and difficulty balancing personal and professional obligations.

As women, we are unique. We are wired to enhance whatever we are connected to. You are a powerful woman, and now is the time for you to embrace and own your Greatness! You can be successful personally and continue to grow professionally. You are capable of making yourself a priority just as much as you consider the needs of those around you. When you stop and think about it, you've made it through your previous experiences of discomfort even when the outcome seemed doubtful. You are more prepared than you realize because you have already overcome other obstacles that have presented themselves against you personally and professionally.

As a professional black woman, I have moved beyond the notion of having to be Superwoman and have no desire to pick up that superhero cape again. I've learned to address my needs in the midst of caring for others, and I have been delivered from the limitations and opinions of others. Paying attention to my personal needs has helped me create balance in my life and resulted in me being more effective professionally. At the age of 26, I graduated with my PhD in Marriage and Family Therapy. As a highly educated, young black woman working in mental health, I was faced with the task of discovering my capabilities while also being responsible for leading others.

Whether it was personally or professionally, I was accustomed to putting the needs of others first because it was what was natural to me—what I had always done. As a new leader, this way of thinking left me hurt, disappointed, and negatively impacted by others. The turning point in my life occurred when I learned not to depend on others for validation or approval. Over the course of time, I started to embrace and find meaning in all aspects of my life, even the uncomfortable parts of my childhood and adult experiences. It became apparent to me that the challenges I encountered were a part of God's greater plan for my life. With this shift in my thinking, I began to view obstacles as opportunities for improvement and growth.

She's a 10: The Black Woman's Guide to Embracing Personal & Professional Greatness was written to remind you of your priceless value as you navigate through life's mountaintop and valley experiences. I hope this book reminds you to make your self-care a priority. If you are running on empty, you will not have the energy to effectively manage the other areas of your life. The time is now. The next level awaits you. You have nothing to lose but everything to gain as you boldly embrace your Greatness.

You're a 10, girl!
Maria Shantell

Most organizations don't realize that negative racial and gender stereotypes are traumatic for those on the receiving end and ultimately limit employee productivity.

She's Aware of Her Trauma

According to Time's Up Foundation,[1] many black women tend to rely on their inner strength and take the path of silence when faced with adverse experiences in life. This reinforces society's unfamiliarity with black women's experiences with trauma. On the other hand, when a black woman chooses to defy the odds and speak out about her traumatic experiences, our society often displays discomfort.

Trauma isn't a foreign concept. To be clear, trauma is anything experienced over the course of your life that has had or is currently having a negative impact on who you

---

[1] "Black Survivors and Sexual Trauma." *TIME'S UP Foundation*, Time's Up, 20 May 2020, timesupfoundation.org/black-survivors-and-sexual-trauma/.

are emotionally, physically, or socially. It is also important to note that sometimes people consciously or subconsciously repress their trauma because the experience was gravely uncomfortable. Trauma can consist of a wide range of events stemming from something as serious as sexual or physical abuse to the passing of a loved one to emotional neglect. While some types of trauma appear simple to overcome to outsiders, they can have just as much of a lasting impact as others commonly discussed. Traumatic events, which can occur at any time in your life, impact how you perceive yourself and others. I believe everyone experiences some form of trauma over the course of their lives.

Because of the "culture of strength" mentality I was raised in, I didn't recognize or accept the rape I had experienced as traumatic until several years after it took place. When it occurred, I was embarrassed that something like that had happened to me. Although I repeatedly said "no" and "stop," I blamed myself because I felt as if I wasn't aggressive enough to prevent my attacker from violating me. I remained silent because I was scared. I feared my loved ones would retaliate against him and end up in jail. I was afraid to fully process what had occurred and relive that painful moment. I remained silent.

Many months after I was raped, I told my mom what had happened. Although I felt relieved to have finally told my story to someone else, fear of what would happen next took hold of me. I asked my mom not to do anything. The next morning after I spoke with my mom, she took a different route home from church. While she drove, I knew she was on a mission to confront my rapist. She entered the store and attentively looked at the name tag of every young male she passed to find the one who hurt me. When she found him, I remained still as I stood by her side. I was terrified to face him again, and I had no idea what my mom would do.

My mom walked up to my attacker and asked him point blank if he raped me. He calmly told her that he did and apologized. It made me sick to my stomach when he said he did it because he really liked me and wanted to be with me. He forced himself on me, despite my petition for him to stop, because he supposedly had feelings for me. The next words out of my mother's mouth left me proud and speechless. She said, "When she comes in this store, if you even look at her, I will kill you." That day, without realizing it, my mother planted a seed that would later be watered and lead to my healing from the trauma I had endured. On the few occasions I did go into the store after that day, my attacker ran the opposite way whenever he saw me.

Even after my mom's involvement and his acknowledgement of sexually assaulting me, I still didn't want to press charges against him because I was in denial about the rape. I didn't want that one incident to define who I was as a person. I didn't want to be a victim forever. After the incident, I went on to successfully complete my undergraduate and graduate studies. Until that point, I had been able to repress what had happened to me years prior. However, I began my career in the mental health field by working with a female client who had experienced sexual abuse. I could no longer run from my past or pretend it didn't exist; I had to come to terms with my own story of sexual abuse.

Personal

When most people hear the word "trauma," they automatically focus on physical or sexual occurrences. Although these aspects of trauma are significant and impactful, one major component of trauma that is not highlighted as often is the emotional damage that is inflicted. For example, emotional trauma during childhood may be reflected in how you were mistreated by a parent or guardian. It may also stem from the absence or loss of a parental figure.

My biological father was absent from my life, but I didn't realize the grave impact of this until I got older. When I was younger, I became accustomed to solving most problems that a male would typically encounter on my own. I didn't have the security of a father growing up, so I was forced to navigate my way through life. I didn't want to go through life with every decision I made carrying significant weight, but it was unavoidable. My reality was that I was a black female who was forced to figure virtually everything out on my own. As a teenager, what some may have considered to be simple tasks, such as carrying heavy items from the car inside the house, became a source of emotional frustration for me. It wasn't emotionally taxing because I was incapable of carrying the items, but it caused me to break down because I was reminded of the void in my life of not having a father to help when I needed it most.

When I began dating, I realized I didn't know how to ask for help because I was accustomed to doing everything myself. The idea of asking for help or being vulnerable with a man made me uncomfortable. I was scared of asking for help and being disappointed. This fear that took root during my childhood caused me to develop a pattern of becoming emotionally disconnected in romantic relationships whenever there was conflict or discomfort. My walls went up as a way of potentially protecting myself from experiencing rejection.

As I matured and had more life experience under my belt, I was placed in positions where I had to learn to face my fear of being rejected. I had to discover how to communicate my vulnerabilities to the opposite sex and deal with any response I was given in a healthy way. Ultimately,

I had to learn not to allow my fear of rejection to keep me from asking for help. This is something I grapple with; I am still on this journey of learning and growing.

Professional

Trauma can also happen as a result of unexpected or uncomfortable workplace conditions. More specifically, black women tend to encounter a variety of trauma-related instances in their work environments that leave lasting imprints on who they are and how they relate to others. In this case, it is important to gain insight regarding your upsetting experience so that you can become consciously aware when specific situations may present themselves in the future. From there, you can choose to not allow your previous experiences to become a stumbling block for you as you continue to grow and develop professionally.

Corporate Challenge #1: Young, Black, Credentialed & Disliked

One challenge that professional black women in the workplace face is mistreatment due to being highly credentialed and younger than their colleagues. Growing up, I didn't see many people actively choosing their professions. Members of my family tended to find employment and stay with a company or in a position for as long as possible.

Since most didn't attend or graduate from college, there weren't many options for upward mobility and advancement. Considering all of this, I was overcome with gratitude when I became the first person in my immediate family to graduate from college.

Although I had tremendous support from family, I had to learn a lot about myself and others as I progressed in my career. The idea of having a career path was new to me because no one around me really seemed to be in a position to decide where they wanted to go or what they wished to do professionally. After spending nine years pursuing my undergraduate and graduate degrees, I received my PhD at the age of 26.

Because of my educational background, I was immediately thrust into major leadership positions when my professional career began. At the time, I didn't necessarily think I was prepared for some of the leadership roles I was given, but many employers and recruiters simply deemed me as qualified because I had the credentials on paper to support their decisions to promote me to higher positions. On one occasion, I went to interview for a therapist position and left with a job offer to work as the program director. This didn't bother me because I have always been open to learning and growing, so I never turned down an opportunity to do so. However, there was a price that I would unknowingly be forced to pay for being an educated black woman in a position of power at such an early age.

One example of workplace trauma that impacts many professional women is being disliked because they are young, black, and credentialed. It took me a long time to realize that my experiences in various workplaces due to my race, gender, and age was trauma. In hindsight, if I had known all that would transpire in the places where I worked, I would have thought twice about accepting those leadership positions or politely walked away from the offers. Despite all of this, I am grateful for the uncomfortable experiences I encountered because I gained an ample amount of wisdom that has helped shape me into a well-rounded leader.

At work, because of my nature, I was optimistic and hopeful. Though I had a lot of energy and genuine intentions when interacting with my colleagues, I was disliked. In one leadership position, I was responsible for managing a large staff of mental health clinicians, educators, medical personnel, and administrators. Many of my staff members initially assumed I was a pushover because of my friendly demeanor and age. They were comfortable and eager to divulge details about their personal lives but, when it came down to meeting the company's goals and objectives, struggled with being held accountable by someone younger in age.

My top priority was to be effective in my role, and my staff understood that. However, many of them did not like it. Some staff members intentionally and overtly challenged my program decisions. Initially, when I became aware of their dislike for me, I questioned myself and my leadership skills. I spent quite a bit of time trying to determine what it was about me that made several of my staff members not like me. Later, I realized that I did not fit the typical stereotype of what they thought a leader should be. I was young, black, a woman, and passionate about my job. My ideas were new and different from what the organization had been doing for many years. Because they were scared of change, they rebelled against anything that represented it, including me.

There were several situations where specific staff members intentionally addressed me by my first name in front of patients and other colleagues. Now, I have never been big on titles, but it began to bother me once I noticed these same staff members never omitted Dr. when referring or speaking to my white counterparts. As this trend continued, I realized that the workplace conflict was bigger than me. Instead of cowering or acquiescing to those staff members, I unapologetically embraced who I was: young, black, and credentialed.

Throughout my career, I've come to realize that experiencing and dealing with workplace conflict has given me wisdom to continue to rise and become a better leader. As I matured in leadership, I stopped questioning myself. The discomfort of others was no longer a stumbling block for me. Instead, it gave me the courage to excel because I knew that several people wanted to see me fail. The bottom line is that you have to own what you do. You have to embrace what makes you, YOU. Once you become comfortable doing so, the people around you will, too.

Corporate Challenge #2: The Angry Black Woman

The next challenge a vast number of professional black women encounter on the job involves unfair judgments and stereotypes that miscategorize them as "angry." In my 14 years of working in the mental health field, I have noticed this common theme among professional black women. A large percentage of black women express having difficulty discussing their true workplace experiences due to the fear of being misunderstood and mislabeled. As a result, even though they are suffering internally, many black women have trained themselves to walk around at work with a poker face to mask their pain. This becomes an uphill battle because black women think they must either be outspoken or remain quietly disgruntled. Regardless, both of these responses lead to black women being labeled as "angry." The unfortunate truth is that a black woman is perceived negatively by others when her emotions are not easily understood, which leaves her feeling stuck. As an attempt to avoid being further misunderstood, most black women take the path of least resistance and silently endure their work related trauma.

I recall working in an organization in which I was all too familiar with being outnumbered. My superiors were passive aggressive and often gave directives to my employees without communicating the same information to me. They intentionally left me out of discussions. When I had conversations with them to address my concerns, they feigned ignorance or behaved as if they were the victims. My attempts to get on the same page or request clarification were met with resistance. Furthermore, I witnessed their passive aggressive behavior through their intentional avoidance and unwillingness to address the issues. Instead of directly dealing with concerns, they often responded to my questions with sarcasm or not at all.

Within my leadership role, I intentionally demonstrated the level of professionalism I expected to receive from my colleagues. However, my approach in addressing problems as they arose resulted in me being labeled an "angry black woman." After carefully studying my surroundings and analyzing the incidents that led to me being given this title, I later realized that two categories of black women existed in the corporate world. The silent black woman never spoke up. She casually went along with every decision made or action taken in an effort to minimize conflict and appease her superiors. She is considered to be the "token black woman." However, even when a black woman carefully and clearly communicates her convictions, she risks being labeled as "angry" by her counterparts.

Upon further reflection, when investigating the root of the issue with my colleagues, I realized one of the other black female supervisor's had the personality of someone considered a "token black woman." She went along with whatever was suggested and never expressed any doubts or concerns regarding the program. Although she had a few side conversations with me about her discomfort, she never spoke up. I believe this limited her effectiveness as a black female in a leadership position. She was unhappy and had concerns about how things were being done in the program, but she suppressed them because she feared how she would be perceived. As a result, because I watched her cower instead of stepping into her role as a black woman in leadership, I intentionally chose not to allow anyone in the office to silence me.

It is not your job to make others understand you because this results in you experiencing unnecessary pressure. When you become silent due to the fear of being characterized inappropriately, it impacts your ability to function at your full potential. Eventually, you will find yourself operating solely based on what others think of you, which will cripple your skills and the value you bring to your company. Most organizations don't realize that negative racial and gender stereotypes are traumatic for those on the receiving end and ultimately limit employee productivity. With this being the case, organizations should equip themselves with a better understanding of the cultural dynamics of African Americans in the workplace.

Corporate Challenge #3: Jealousy from Other Women

Another crippling issue that impacts many professional black women in the workplace is jealousy from other women. I was one of the few minorities in my master's program at the private Christian university I attended. During my second year of the program, I was responsible for completing a high number of client contact hours to gain more practical experience in the field of mental health. I loved working with clients and was accustomed to being in my own lane, so I didn't realize that I had completed my client contact hours before my classmates.

Unaware that there was an issue, I began to notice that some of my classmates started becoming distant. When I walked into the room, they would immediately stop talking. One day, I walked into class and the professor stated that she had witnessed the way my classmates' behaviors toward me had changed. She even went so far as to say it was because I was excelling in the program. After her speech, several of my classmates apologized to me and expressed that they had been jealous of how well I was doing in the program. I was overwhelmed and completely caught off guard as to how many of them felt toward me. I accepted their apologies.

While in graduate school, I had a roommate and would randomly do nice things for her. After a couple months of her moving in I noticed she had difficulty affording basic necessities. I proceeded to make her a large gift basket filled with items she needed like a shower curtain, bathroom decor, snacks, and other quality items. Additionally, I would regularly invite her to grab lunch or to work out, but she would tell me that she had other plans. After several months of turning down my invitations, my roommate informed me that she felt convicted and wanted to apologize for being jealous of me. After our transparent conversation, her previous interactions with me began to make sense. I accepted her apology.

Although I was able to move past both of these incidents and forgive my classmates and roommate, I had to ask myself how I contributed to them feeling jealous of me. Soon, I began questioning my interactions with others and thinking that I needed to pull back from social situations. After these experiences, I struggled with embracing who

~ ~

I was fully because of the fear that I would make others uncomfortable. Without realizing it, I started to have trauma-related responses in association with these experiences and allowed the limitations of others to define me.

Jealousy among women in professional settings is quite common. One would think that women would naturally support one another in professional settings because they are not always given the same opportunities as men. However, jealousy in the workplace prevents many women from coming alongside another woman in leadership and helping her thrive, which can be a major source of trauma. It is common to hear black women in leadership positions discuss their encounters with jealous white women. However, it is not as often that black women have open dialogue concerning their experiences with jealous black women.

Throughout my work experiences in a variety of settings, I have encountered uncomfortable situations with black and white women. The situations that caught me off guard the most were those with other black women. As a minority, I learned early in my professional career that not all white people respected and accepted my role as a leader. Additionally, I expected early on that I would naturally receive more support from other professional black women because we may have possibly gone through similar obstacles associated with working in the corporate world. Sadly, this was a false expectation.

In one of my first major leadership positions after being officially done with school, I was tasked with leading several departments. I was particularly excited and hopeful because many of the individuals I was responsible for supervising were black. I was eager to help other black women become better leaders. However, I encountered a disconcerting amount of drama. After spending some time getting to know me, my supervisor, a well-rounded white woman, had a transparent conversation with me. She told me that she initially believed I was the source of the drama and confusion that unfolded when I first started in my role managing the program. She went on to explain that, after carefully observing everyone, she finally realized the other black women there were attempting to sabotage me. She told me about the emails she received from one of the employees I supervised stating that she didn't like how I operated the program and that I also would come to work unprofessionally dressed.

Even though I appreciated my supervisor's candor in speaking with me, because I knew it came from a sincere place, I was hurt. Hearing a white woman share her observations regarding the other black women in the workplace giving me a hard time caused me a significant amount of pain. It hurt to have a white woman ask me why the other black women were attempting to sabotage me, another black woman. I was unable to answer my supervisor's question because there was nothing that I could say to reduce the pain and disappointment I felt at that time. As a professional black woman, I was embarrassed. My supervisor ended the conversation by telling me her thoughts about the matter. After observing everything, she stated that she had witnessed other women compliment me on my work attire and concluded that some colleagues were only giving me a hard time because they were jealous of me.

After that conversation with my supervisor, I knew I had to maintain sincere interactions with my colleagues. It gave me peace knowing that I hadn't done anything to contribute to their dislike for me. I continued in my role as their supervisor without letting on that I knew they secretly wanted me gone. The unfortunate thing is that a lot of black women struggle with celebrating or making room for other black women in professional environments. Unfortunately, some black women view each other as competition and many feel threatened in the presence of other successful black women. The truth is, there is more than enough room at the table for us as black women to shine while sharing our gifts, talents, and abilities with one another.

I know without a doubt that my previous graduate school experiences equipped me to better deal with jealousy from others in the workplace. I realized the disdain aimed at me had nothing to do with who I was. Instead, it was a reflection of the insecurities held by those who hurled insults at me. It wasn't my responsibility to address their insecurities or give attention to them. I was only responsible for how I responded and interacted with my peers. The key is to shine being who you are despite what other people think about you.

CHAPTER 1:

She's Aware of Her Trauma

Practical Application - Your Path to Greatness

Reflect on the areas in your life that have caused you trauma.

1. *In what areas of your personal life have you experienced trauma (the passing of a loved one, abuse, emotional neglect, etc.)?*

   ____

   ____

   ____

   ____

2. *In what areas of your professional life have you experienced trauma?*

   ____

   ____

   ____

   ____

3. *How do your personal and workplace experiences with trauma impact the way you currently live your life?*

____

____

____

____

____

____

____

____

The "Superwoman mentality" is one of the most unhealthy threats to black women because it creates a false image that negatively impacts our ability to process our emotions and cripples our interactions with others.

CHAPTER TWO

She Tosses Her Superwoman Cape

As a black woman, I often felt as if I always had to have everything together. To this day, my mom, grandmother, and aunts are immaculate at being caretakers and overall great at ensuring my family members are well taken care of. They married, cook great food, have raised multiple kids, and juggle regular household tasks all while working outside of their homes. Growing up surrounded by "strong" women, I also watched them trying to save the world while attempting to avoid discussing any uncomfortable emotions they felt. Witnessing this, I became familiar with and eventually adopted a similar outlook. I grew up believing that, as a black woman, it was my responsibility to keep it all together and not discuss anything that would make me appear weak or vulnerable.

My mom raised five kids, started several businesses, and always made time to learn something new. Despite the strong sense of pride I felt while I watched my mother work, as a young girl, I also recall her not making much time for herself. Looking back, I have no idea how she juggled all of her responsibilities. She always appeared to have a plan despite the obstacles that came her way. As I matured, I realized I adopted the same mindset. I assumed my role as a black woman was to be Superwoman and manage as many tasks as possible while neglecting my own physical, emotional, and mental health needs. The "Superwoman mentality" is one of the most unhealthy threats to black women because it creates a false image that negatively impacts our ability to process our emotions and cripples our interactions with others.

When my sweet sister, Alicia, passed away on May 20, 2019, it felt as if a part of me had died with her. For the first time in my life, I felt completely helpless and was forced to acknowledge my discomfort because the pain of losing her was unbearable. Six months prior to her passing, I was heavily involved in advocating on her behalf at the hospital in Louisiana. After a six-month battle and working with a news station on a story about the hospital's negligence in her treatment, she was finally airlifted to a different hospital in Boston with doctors who specialized in treating her rare disease. Once she was in Boston receiving treatment, I felt like I could finally breathe because I had spent the six months prior with her in the hospital every day pleading and hoping that her treating physicians in Baton Rouge would eventually provide her access to the specialized medical care she needed. After being in Boston for five days, my sister passed away because she didn't receive the vital treatment she needed quickly enough.

Alicia's death hit me hard. I had been prayerful and persistent throughout her journey. I made sure my family was encouraged and hopeful because I really believed, deep down, that she was going to live. Her passing completely knocked me down to the point that I was no longer able to manage my other responsibilities. I stepped away from participating in community organizations and stopped giving my time and energy to family and friends who took me for granted. I was forced to put myself first and put down my superwoman cape. I didn't have the energy or motivation to focus on what other people needed from me because I was no longer capable of being everything to everyone. As strong as I was accustomed to being, I didn't have the energy anymore.

Deep down inside, I questioned God and why He took my sister at such a young age. I questioned why she didn't have access to the proper treatment for her initial six-month hospital stay. I wondered why she wasn't given the opportunity to see her dream of opening her own daycare come to fruition. I asked God why He would allow her only child, Kameron, to grow up without her. Without realizing it, I had lost all hope. I had even accepted that God might decide to take me at a young age, too. Along with that thought came the notion that I could leave earth without having the husband and kids that I desired. All of these thoughts left me feeling stuck, hurt, sad, and listless. I realized I was not Superwoman and accepted that I was merely human.

In my personal and professional interactions with others, I was accustomed to successfully solving problems. I was also familiar with showing up for and being present with the people around me. Unable and unwilling to do for myself, my sister's passing forced me to allow others to be there for me. Professionally, I became more vulnerable with my colleagues, which unknowingly resulted in more growth in their lives. I also became okay with realizing that I had to embrace the uncomfortable parts of my inner self and I learned to own my struggles. I realized my real strength was revealed in my moments of weakness, not when things appeared picture perfect in my life.

Putting down my superwoman cape gave me a freedom I had never experienced before, and my perspective on life changed. When you go through unforeseen obstacles in life, you have to remember that you are human. Do not place unrealistic expectations on yourself because they can lead to unexpressed emotions that can delay your healing journey. Once you come to terms with and accept your human limitations, those around you will follow suit. Take the pressure off yourself. Take off the cape. Be who you are even in moments of difficulty.

Once I took off my superwoman cape, I no longer felt pressured to give in to false realities or expectations. When my sister passed, I was forced to completely put down my superwoman cape. Now, I have absolutely no desire to pick it back up.

CHAPTER 2:

She Tosses Her Superwoman Cape

Practical Application - Your Path to Greatness

1. ***Do you hold on to the notion that you must be Superwoman? How do you think it developed?***

    ____

    ____

    ____

    ____

    ____

2. ***How do you feel about sharing your vulnerabilities with others?***

    ____

    ____

    ____

    ____

3. *How has your desire to be Superwoman negatively impacted you personally and professionally?*

As you walk by faith, your core beliefs and value system will always keep you grounded and focused on what matters most.

CHAPTER THREE

She Walks by Faith

When a house is being built, a lot of time is spent ensuring the foundational pieces are in their proper place. The builders usually devote a large amount of time laying the foundation because, once that is established, the remaining components of the home usually go up pretty quickly. The same concept applies to your spiritual walk. Your foundation is what will keep you grounded when you encounter good and difficult moments in life.

Growing up, church was a major part of my life. Raised in a traditional Baptist church, I attended Sunday school, Bible study, and Sunday service each week. Although I went to church regularly, I did not know God for myself. It wasn't until I was 18 years old that I developed a personal relationship with God.

⁂

While in college, I worked part time in the floral department of a local grocery store. I remember being positively influenced by a supervisor who was genuine in her interactions with others. One day, she invited me to a women's empowerment conference at her church. I accepted the invitation and told my mom about the event. Weeks later, upon entering the church to attend the conference, I was in awe when I saw people worshipping God. Everyone appeared happy and free as they danced and clapped their hands. This was totally different from what I had experienced growing up, so it became the catalyst for me to learn more about God.

As a young girl, I always thought there was more to God than what I had been exposed to. Being at my supervisor's church sparked something in me, so I began attending Sunday services there. After some time, I joined the church and developed a thirst to learn and grow in the things of God. It was at this point that I began to understand the power that came with having a relationship with God.

Once I began to understand who God was for myself, I no longer had a desire to hang around certain people. It wasn't because they were bad or I thought I was better than them. I simply realized that our priorities in life were different. I became more sensitive to God's spirit and His plans and purpose for my life. As I grew deeper in my faith,

I started to feel discomfort when I did things that went against the Holy Spirit's leading.

I used to regularly communicate with a male friend before leaving for college. Even though I knew I needed to cut off communication with him, I continued talking with him. The more we spoke, the more unsettled I felt. Eventually, I made the decision to stop communicating with him and end the relationship. The decision to cut off my friend was not one that I took lightly, especially because he regularly expressed his desire to have a future with me. However, I later learned why I felt the urge to walk away. This young man was older and often said that he didn't want me to go away to school. My lack of peace was God protecting me from potentially staying with him and preventing me from going down the path of not living out His purpose for my life. If I hadn't gone away to school, I would not be the woman I am today because I would have missed out on the character-building and professional opportunities I have had. I thank God for speaking to me about this relationship because, as a result of me ending things, I have been able to help and walk alongside countless people on their own journeys.

Giving a lot of energy and time to others around me has always been a part of my nature. I remember feeling overwhelmed and disappointed my junior year of college because I gave so much to others but did not get much in return. One evening, I was extremely disappointed because of this and fell to my knees in prayer in the middle of my apartment. As I cried out to God, I knew I didn't have to go into detail because He already knew the sadness in my heart. On this particular night, I was emotionally transparent with God. For the first time in my spiritual life as I cried profusely, I clearly heard the voice of God. In the midst of me ugly crying on my knees, He said, "Don't worry about what others don't do for you. Concern yourself with what I do for you." Immediately, a sense of peace came over me. From that moment on, I developed a new perspective. Even in the midst of me giving and doing nice things for others, my expectations of what God was capable of doing for me increased.

Shifting my focus to what God could do for me, I accepted that my big heart was a gift to the world. I realized that I couldn't expect everyone I encountered to be considerate because many people do not have that gift. God has equipped each of us with special gifts and talents. After realizing I was a giver, I began harnessing my energy in assisting others in developing solutions to their problems. That experience showed me that my needs are met through God, not through people. He doesn't require me to have all the answers but to only take one step at a time and trust His leading.

God became even more pivotal in my professional life as I began incorporating Him into my everyday activities.

Starting my day early with prayer and positive thinking helped me to navigate moments of great difficulty and adversity. The first hour of my day was spent reading scriptures and listening to uplifting music. I found words in the Bible that were similar to the situations I faced and used them as a source of hope each day. Because several of my leadership positions were in high-conflict work environments, I was able to maintain my composure and peace as I focused my energy on a purpose that was bigger than me. By doing so, I was reminded that the discomfort I was experiencing was only temporary. My co-workers often complimented me on my demeanor, but I knew that I wouldn't have been able to handle myself with grace if I had not spiritually prepared each day before I went to work and trusted God to lead me.

Years ago, I was hired by a multi million dollar corporation to assist with strategy and implementation of mental health initiatives. Once again, I was the outcast because I was one of the few black women in leadership who happened to not be from that region. As a result, I knew I had to utilize wisdom and depend on the Holy Spirit at all times while at work. As someone in leadership, I recognized that some of the policies and practices were not in the best interest of the population being served.

Thinking about my morals, passion for the population being served, and professional code of conduct gave me the courage to address many of the questionable operating procedures that had become a part of the organizational culture. I feared having to walk down an unknown path alone. I dreaded the possibility of being misunderstood. Because I had to make difficult decisions and perform unfavorable tasks, some co-workers tried to malign me or set me up for defeat. On one occasion, an employee fabricated a story and falsely reported an incident in which she claimed another employee had sexually abused a minor client. After a thorough investigation, it was discovered that her claims of sexual abuse committed by another employee were unfounded. In my role, I was then responsible for terminating her.

As if I did not have enough to deal with, a police officer came to my office the next day after I had terminated the employee who had made the false claim to inform me that the same person had reported that I had physically assaulted her. Before the officer set foot in my office, the Holy Spirit told me to remain calm. By the grace of God, the officer explained that he knew that the employee's claims needed to be verified because she had a history of making false reports against others. The officer suggested that I file a report against her because she had attempted to seek revenge because I was the one who had terminated her employment. Considering the circumstances, I offered her grace and did not press charges because her malevolent attempt to hurt me backfired. God showed up to protect me.

After enduring the uncomfortable experience of being maliciously slandered, I became a trailblazer within the organization. For the remainder of my time there, I began to notice other people in leadership positions who had worked in silence for many years start to speak up and report their own instances of injustice. If I had not relied on the Holy Spirit for guidance and strength during that time, others may not have had the courage to speak up about the challenges they witnessed or faced.

Your uncomfortable experiences are not just about you. Oftentimes, your discomfort has a purpose that's bigger than you. Maybe you're only meant to work at your job for a season to usher in change and shift the atmosphere. While doing so, the key is to trust God as much as possible throughout your discomfort because something bigger than you keeps you focused. It reminds you that you have a purpose and gives you instructions when you're frustrated or feel weak.

Many people wonder how I've made it through high-conflict work environments. The secret has always been my faith walk. My secret weapon has been my ability to shift my faulty way of thinking and completely rely on God and His plans for my life. In doing so, He has provided me with wisdom and specific instructions during some of the most uncomfortable experiences of my life. As you walk by faith, your core beliefs and value system will always keep you grounded and focused on what matters most.

Don't be too hard on yourself if you're only able to spend a few minutes here or there with God. Sometimes, we have unrealistic expectations that only prevent us from being consistent in how much time we spend with Him. Talk to Him because He understands. Like any other relationship, our relationship with God requires communication. He wants you to tell Him when you're overwhelmed, tired, frustrated, or even disappointed. Some people believe that God must not be questioned. However, in some of my most uncomfortable moments in life, I have discovered that He desires full transparency. Our relationship with Him improves when we're honest even during our moments of discomfort.

CHAPTER 3:

She Walks by Faith

Practical Application - Your Path to Greatness

1. ***What specific things would you like to implement in your faith walk to help you grow spiritually?***

____

____

____

____

____

2. ***What gifts or talents has God given you?***

____

____

____

____

____

3. *Think back to some of your difficult moments in life. How did God protect you?*

For the professional black woman who often has to juggle numerous hats and is unable to allocate sufficient time to her own self-care, trying to be perfect can become crippling.

CHAPTER FOUR

She Gives Herself Grace for Improvement

I believe a lot of high-achieving professional black women struggle with perfectionism. While working with this particular demographic, I have come to realize that perfectionism is one of the main sources of anxiety plaguing professional black women. Attempts to do things perfectly can cause you to spend unnecessary time and energy on tasks that usually lead to further worry, guilt, and fear. For the professional black woman who often has to juggle numerous hats and is unable to allocate sufficient time to her own self-care, trying to be perfect can become crippling.

Before I opened my business, I spent a lot of time thinking things had to be perfect. I became consumed by the small details. However, I realized spending energy on striving for perfection only delayed me further. My desire for perfection distracted me from making the progress I desired. Instead of striving for perfection, I realized I accomplished more when I did my best and showed myself grace when I missed the mark.

There is a freedom that comes with accepting that you are human and will sometimes error. Usually in life, the most growth occurs during those times when we mess up or make mistakes. There is a strength that comes when you accept your personal limitations. This increases your emotional intelligence and teaches you to show grace to others when they need it as well.

Many professional black women regularly choose to stay busy to prevent themselves from acknowledging or accepting when they have missed the mark. I believe this "functional busyness" is why black women are one of the most successful groups of individuals. We have learned to focus our attention on the professional accomplishments that we can control. However, we haven't learned the concept of showing grace to ourselves. The more you allow yourself to own your personal limitations, the more you progress in life. In my years of providing mental health counseling to others, I have discovered that most people who are in denial about their limitations are the ones who tend to struggle the most internally.

After nine years of schooling, I felt completely lost once I was no longer a student. It was almost as if school was a fantasy world that kept me consumed with crushing goals and seeing immediate progress. School was where I could consume myself with studying and immediately score an A on a test. I was comfortable operating on a deadline-driven schedule because I could somewhat control the outcome. It was as if my behavior in school provided me with instant gratification.

My success in school made me believe I had to have the same level of control in my life to achieve success after graduation. I thought I could control the outcome of everything I did if I just gave it my all. After graduate school, I attempted to apply the same immediate gratification philosophy to other areas of my life, but I struggled. As you go through life, you may come to the realization that difficult moments are beyond your control. Your efforts to overachieve or control areas of your life only prevent you from facing reality. This way of thinking eventually wore me out, but it also taught me to embrace my shortcomings.

CHAPTER 4:

She Gives Herself Grace for Improvement

Practical Application - Your Path to Greatness

1. *List 3 ways you can currently show grace to yourself.*

____

____

____

____

____

2. *What is the biggest hindrance that prevents you from embracing your mistakes?*

____

____

____

____

3. *How has the desire for perfectionism impacted your life?*

A black woman who embraces greatness knows her worth and understands that every area of her life has purpose.

She's Intentional by Any Means Necessary

Compared to their white counterparts, professional black women tend to have a higher rate of being single. Research from Yale University found that educated black women, in comparison to white women with similar education backgrounds, are twice as likely to have never been married by age 45.[2] Additionally, professional black women also tend to marry later in life. I believe a major part of this phenomenon is due to the intentionality of black women in pursuing successful careers. Furthermore, a large number of educated black women have learned the

[2] "Marriage, Family on the Decline for Highly Educated Black Women." *YaleNews*, Yale, 9 Aug. 2009, news.yale.edu/2009/08/08/marriage-family-decline-highly-educated-black-women.

importance of applying that same level of intentionality to their personal lives. A black woman who embraces greatness knows her worth and understands that every area of her life has purpose. She understands that all things work for her good even if it means she has to patiently wait for a compatible life partner with similar values and goals.

Personally, I never imagined that I would be single in my 30s. Having a family of my own has always been just as important to me as having a successful career. Because I grew up in a large family, I always had a desire to have a big family of my own one day. Truthfully, I was so focused during my time in school that I didn't date much. For me, it was important to approach dating with the same intentionality as I did my career.

My love life could have probably flourished if I had stayed put in one place and settled down. Regardless, I wanted to ensure I maximized the opportunities presented to me, so I had no problem pursuing training opportunities in Louisiana, Texas, Michigan, Canada, and DC. I've always desired to meet someone and fall in love. However, I also believed that my love life was pre-orchestrated by God. I knew I couldn't just carelessly marry someone just to get married. I had seen so many people around me do that, then end up miserable and unhappy. I wanted my story to be different.

My desire is to have a purposeful marriage in which

my future husband and I will help each other grow and become better individuals. I want my marriage to be a blessing to others. Knowing I wasn't created to carelessly marry, I remain determined to continue living out my purpose until I meet a man I believe I should marry. I would be lying if I said that life as a single, professional black woman is easy. During my moments of loneliness and frustration, I remind myself of why I choose not to settle for just any man. I know my value, and I know what I deserve. I know the times when I've had to be obedient in ending relationships due to the other person not being part of God's purpose for my life.

Many professional black women experience difficulty when dating. I've heard countless black women say they believe that men are often intimidated by their success. Many of these same women also believe that success didn't just randomly bump them in the head; they have acknowledged their success was the product of them being intentional about pursuing what they desired. If you identify with this, I would like to encourage you to continue being intentional in your personal and professional efforts despite how you are perceived by others. You are of high value. One day, if it is God's will, you will connect with a man that is just as intentional as you are. Do not allow the misconceptions of others to hinder you.

Most people who don't know me think that my career

is the focus of my life. The truth is my family life is more important than my career. I pursue my career in the manner that I do so that I can have freedom to enjoy my family. I wanted the freedom to not have to request off from work to attend my future children's school activities. I desire the freedom to spend as much time at home as I would like. I have intentionally created a career without restrictions to spend time with my future husband and kids exactly the way I want to.

There are many black women, such as myself, who have always desired a family. It's not that marriage hasn't been a priority. Rather, it's just that, as professional black women, we're taught to be intentional about what we want. The average man may not understand the desire of your heart or your "why." It is your responsibility to make sure that the men you date understand and support your pursuits. If not, it can lead to frustration and you second guessing your Greatness.

CHAPTER 5:

She's Intentional by Any Means Necessary

Practical Application - Your Path to Greatness

1. ***Share 2 ways you have been intentional in your professional efforts.***

   ____

   ____

   ____

   ____

2. ***What is your WHY, or reason for your pursuits, that keeps you grounded in your personal life?***

   ____

   ____

   ____

   ____

If you allow it to, fear will keep you trapped in a box of comfort. It is only during those moments of pushing past your discomfort that you will grow and overcome fear.

CHAPTER SIX

She Overcomes Fear

After 14 years of working with diverse groups of individuals, I have come to realize how common fear is. More specifically, I have realized that professional black women have the tendency to suffer in silence when it comes to fear. If you allow it, fear can impact every area of your life. Fear-based thinking is usually the result of previous negative experiences that continue to restrain how you live.

It wasn't until I entered adulthood that I realized how fear-based thinking had been a part of my thought process growing up. As a child, something as simple as me sitting in the living room and hearing someone knock on my aunt's door caused me to worry. My mom told me that I often cried in the grocery store whenever she took a few steps away from me and I couldn't see her. I can reflect on other memories during childhood associated with me imagining something bad happening to myself or one of my loved ones.

I have always been in tune with my environment and the people in it. I believe a major part of the development of fear in my life was due to the high-conflict environment in which I was raised because there was often fighting and arguments. I remember a neighbor running into my house with a gun when I was 11 years old and the feeling of helplessness that engulfed me. I recall sitting in the front yard crying and pulling the rollers out of my hair because fear had already caused me to think one of my family members would get hurt. Although nothing happened, I was bombarded with feelings of worry and nervousness about the horrible things that could have happened.

Fear can be crippling and cause you to be consumed with the "what ifs" of life. It can cause your body and emotions to respond as if the situation you envisioned has already occurred although it hasn't. Fear causes you to focus on the future rather than the present. Because fear can control how you think, it may make you tired from overthinking and analyzing. Fear is truly **f**alse **e**vidence **a**ppearing **r**eal. It will make a believer out of you based on the false evidence that develops in your mind. Fear can impact you personally and professionally and make you give unnecessary energy to things that are not worth your focus.

Personally, I have seen fear cause people who sincerely desired close relationships with others to push them away because they were afraid of being hurt. You may have experienced some disappointments in your relationships with others. You may even worry about being hurt or disappointed in the future. If you don't allow yourself to experience life, you will never live it. If you allow it to, fear will keep you trapped in a box of comfort. It is only during those moments of pushing past your discomfort that you will grow and overcome fear.

Professionally, I have seen people stay at dead-end jobs that made them unhappy because they feared the unknown. When I first started my business, I was terrified. I was comfortable with the paycheck I received from my corporate job because I knew exactly how much money I would make each month. Although I wasn't being challenged at work, I was comfortable. Honestly, working for myself full-time has been the most rewarding experience. God knew that He had to make me uncomfortable at my previous job in order for me to start my own business.

If you're experiencing the same discomfort over and over again, chances are you are missing the lesson in the discomfort. God knew I had to experience turmoil in various workplace environments in order for me to become fearless. He knew that, for me to overcome fear, I had to learn how to effectively manage conflict in diverse working environments. By nature, I am a peacemaker, so I didn't have the skills to navigate high-conflict environments. As a result, unknowingly I needed help developing in that area. I would be lying if I said that fear completely left my life. Nevertheless, I have become stronger when fear attempts to present itself. I am also more aware about the thoughts and emotions that I allow to live in my mind.

You, too, have the ability to combat fear. Overcoming fear is a daily process that requires intentional effort. You must first be honest with yourself about the areas in your life in which fear has repeatedly attempted to control. It is also a good idea to share the specific areas that fear has attempted to gain access with your support system. This will help remind you of your greatness and prevent you from feeling alone. You may have to talk back to fear and be intentional in how you battle fear-filled thoughts. It doesn't happen overnight, but you can and will overcome fear!

CHAPTER 6:

She Overcomes Fear

Practical Application - Your Path to Greatness

1. *List 3 fear-based thoughts that have attempted to control your life.*

____

____

____

____

____

2. *Share 1 major life lesson you have learned that came in the form of repeated discomfort.*

____

____

____

____

3. *When you encounter fear, how should you respond?*

Each experience you have in life is like a puzzle piece. Although you only get one piece at a time, one experience at a time, you're eventually able to put them together to create a bigger picture.

She Thinks Big

It's easy to think small. When you think small, you operate in your comfort zone. However, when you're being stretched, you are forced to become uncomfortable. Sometimes, God makes us uncomfortable to adjust our thinking so that we can rely more on Him. Take a moment and think back to a time in your life when you were the most uncomfortable. It probably was also the time that you experienced the most growth. Right?

Although I was raised in one of the worst neighborhoods in Baton Rouge, as a little girl, I always had big dreams. Hearing gunshots and witnessing drug-related activity was a normal part of life for me. I could have easily used the environment where I was raised as an excuse to pursue other things in life. However, over the course of my life, I learned to let my upbringing serve as my motivation to pursue Greatness. I desired a different kind of life for myself, and I know that is one of the reasons why I have encountered so much turmoil. I believe big obstacles are intended to launch us further into our purpose.

As a young girl, I asked God to bless me so that I could be a blessing to others. Sometimes, you have to be careful what you ask for because you just might get it. I believe, because of my childhood desire to be a blessing to others, God has orchestrated my life to fulfill that purpose. By nature, I enjoy helping others in any way that I can. During those times in my life when I have been overwhelmed by giving to others and not getting anything in return, I have reminded myself of my request to God when I was younger. There is a cost associated with having big dreams. The obstacles you face are only preparation for you to receive what you've dreamed of.

When you have big dreams, it can be scary because those desires may seem impossible. It's natural for you to want to rely on your own skills and abilities. However, thinking **big** requires you to step outside of your capabilities. That's when God comes in. He gives you grand desires so that you have to rely on Him to see them come to pass. This is the very reason why it's hard for most people to think big. It's easier to just rely on your own way of thinking than to allow God to stretch you beyond your comfort zone.

Throughout my life, I've had some uncomfortable experiences. However, I have always felt as if they were somehow part of a bigger plan even when I didn't quite understand. I always had a desire to be my own boss. I knew that God had given me a vision to impact the lives of others on a greater level than what I was able to do working for someone else. Because of this desire, I found myself in high-conflict work environments where I had to learn how to depend on Him, not my own abilities. I grew up not liking conflict; my natural way of interacting with others was to avoid conflict as much as possible. God knew this, so He dropped me in high-conflict work environments where He knew that He could produce His best out of me.

Thinking back to some of my past experiences, I realize that God was delivering me from the opinions and limitations of other people. That's the best thing that He could have ever done because it expanded my thinking. Each experience you have in life is like a puzzle piece. Although you only get one piece at a time, one experience at a time, you're eventually able to put them together to create a bigger picture. That's how God works. He places us in one situation at a time as He develops our character and skill set. God knows that if He gave us the whole puzzle at once, most of us would become overwhelmed and not even attempt to do anything with it.

I understand now that my unfortunate experiences were used to shape my thinking. Also, my experiences and everything I've been through in the corporate world taught me how not to treat others.They were essential tools used to help me navigate life. When we think BIG, it is our way of telling God that we trust Him to bring our desires to pass.

Oftentimes, we limit God when we think small. We don't even realize that we limit what He's able to do in our lives. Think BIG, get uncomfortable, and embrace change because those things will launch you to a higher level. When you look back one day, all of those uncomfortable experiences will make sense.

CHAPTER 7:

She Thinks Big

Practical Application - Your Path to Greatness

1. *Share 1 BIG dream you have.*

____

____

____

____

____

2. *What keeps you pushing toward your BIG dream?*

____

____

____

____

____

3. *List 2 things you have learned from your personal or professional obstacles so far.*

You're human, so you will have moments in life when you're not okay. It really is okay not to be okay.

CHAPTER EIGHT

She Realizes It's Okay Not to be Okay

Most of us as black women don't really know what it means to not be okay. I include myself because I can identify with the statement. As black women, we often try to keep things together. However, a major component of being human is realizing that we will have moments in life when we're not okay.

I once worked with a client who had experienced a great deal of trauma. She prided herself on her ability to appear as though she always had everything together, even in those moments when she didn't. Externally, she looked okay but, internally, she was suffering. This was the very thing that was delaying her healing, and she had spent years not realizing it.

One day, I put some chicken patties in the oven. As I was removing them, I hit my arm on the top part of the oven, leaving a long scar on my arm. Before my wound could get better, it went through a process of healing. It bubbled up with pus before the dead skin eventually fell off. Since my arm hurt when I bumped it against any surface, I treated the impacted area to help it heal faster. After some time, my arm no longer hurt as new skin grew in.

Similar to how my arm had to go through its healing process, we must be willing to acknowledge when we are hurt or injured. If I had remained in denial about my arm not being bruised, the healing process would have been delayed because I would not have given my arm the care it needed to heal. You will take a lot of pressure off of yourself when you realize that you will have moments in life when you will not be okay. You're human. The key is to acknowledge when you're not okay so that you can give yourself what you need to become okay. If you always try to keep everything together, you will delay healing and growth in areas that could be beneficial to you.

I had a client share with me that her biggest breakthrough occurred during our time together. She said our therapy sessions were the only times when she gave herself permission to not be okay. She also shared that therapy taught her how to be vulnerable in admitting her shortcomings and not living in pretense. By giving herself permission to not be okay, she also realized it reduced the unrealistic pressure that others placed on her outside of therapy.

It's during moments of acknowledging your weaknesses that your true strength is revealed. My client learned that accepting her shortcomings enabled her to better take care of herself. She was able to create space to do some of the things that she needed to do, such as getting massages and scheduling alone time. When you realize you're not okay, it helps you strategize and plan for what you need. You're human, so you will have moments in life when you're not okay. It really is okay not to be okay. The key is to recognize when you're not okay so that you can implement what's needed to help you release in a healthy way and move forward in the direction of becoming okay.

CHAPTER 8:

She Realizes It's Okay Not to be Okay

Practical Application - Your Path to Greatness

1. *When was the last time you were not okay?*

____

____

____

____

____

2. *List 3 things that help you feel better when you're not okay.*

____

____

____

____

3. *What unrealistic pressures do others place on you?*

Having the right support system makes life easier. The right friends will remind you to take care of yourself during moments when you forget.

CHAPTER NINE

She Has a Solid Support System

Most people are naturally uncomfortable with leaning on others for support because of past disappointments. Furthermore, many black women have a difficult time expressing their vulnerabilities and asking for help. Having the right support system makes it easier to be vulnerable and ask for help when you need it. The right friends will remind you that they are there for you. Life circumstances may have made you falsely believe that you have to figure everything out yourself and not depend on anyone, or you may have built walls up that make it difficult to trust others. Regardless of the situation, it's important to know that getting support is vital for you to achieve Greatness.

I had a client who had difficulty forming connections with others. She was consumed by the thought that no one could be trusted. Because of this thinking, she continued to consistently encounter people she couldn't trust. It was almost as if her expectations were a magnet that caused untrustworthy people to be drawn to her.

You have the ability to determine the kind of individuals you attract. If you think other people around you can't be trusted, those are the types of people you will attract. Some people are trustworthy. The truth is, sometimes you have to make adjustments within yourself to heal before you can connect with those people who are genuinely there to help you in life. Will you allow yourself to become vulnerable enough to let them in?

One of the worst mistakes you can make is to live life alone because it blocks your blessings. You are only one person, and it is impossible for you to embrace Greatness by yourself. John Donne's Meditation XVII explains perfectly the idea of us needing one another: "No man is an island, entire of itself; every man is a piece of the Continent, a part of the main."[3] We were created to be interconnected, so we need to give and receive support. Every major milestone I have accomplished in my life has been the result of having a few solid friends and family members with me

[3] Donne, John, 1572-1631. Devotions Upon Emergent Occasions. Cambridge, [Eng.] :The University press, 1923.

on my journey. You may think you don't have anyone who supports you, but that may not be the case. Think about whether you are supportive of others. Oftentimes, many people don't get support from others because they haven't learned how to be supportive of others.

People who are good at connecting and building relationships with others often understand the concept of what it means to be a friend. They feel good about themselves and, in turn, do their best to help those around them. You will attract what you are. If you want dependable friends, you must first learn to be a dependable friend. As you mature, you realize it's not the quantity of your friendships that matters; it's the quality. In order to have quality friends, you must be a good friend. I once heard it said that if you look at the people that are closest to you, you will see yourself.

Most people don't realize that the individuals they connect with are reflections of themselves. The question is: What type of people do you have in your immediate circle? Are they people you can trust? Are they people who support you? Having the right support system makes life easier. The right friends will remind you to take care of yourself during moments when you forget. When I think of the good times in my life, my friends have been there. When I think of the bad times in my life, my friends have been in my corner holding me up when I've been weak.You should have a support system that knows how to encourage and celebrate you when you need it.

Accountability is another component of having a solid support system that is often overlooked. It is important to be held accountable by trustworthy people who know you and have your best interest at heart. Accountability can put you back on the right path when you feel like you've gotten off track, are confused, or feel stuck. There's no way to grow professionally without growing personally, so utilize the people who have been strategically placed around you for help.

When I was experiencing a great deal of difficulty in the workplace, I felt stuck and confused because I knew that I had the right intentions in my role of supervising others. First, I attempted to go to my boss, who was the CEO of the company, and get feedback from him. I ended up disappointed because he didn't provide me with the feedback that I needed. I knew I needed wisdom and accountability from someone who knew me personally. I wanted to understand not only how I could improve, but also how I could understand the deeper meaning of some of the experiences that I had. I scheduled a meeting with my pastor because he had a lot of experience working in the corporate world. He not only listened as I shared my uncomfortable experiences, but he also gave me in-depth feedback and clarity. My pastor's support and guidance helped me to use wisdom in terms of what I shared and how I shared it in professional environments.

Sometimes you need the perspective of someone you trust, who may not be directly connected to your situation. You should intentionally surround yourself with quality people who can make investments in your life. Don't allow your previous encounters with disappointment to prevent you from experiencing the next level in your life personally and professionally.

CHAPTER 9:

She Has a Solid Support System

Practical Application - Your Path to Greatness

1. *Who are the 3 people closest to you, and what value do they add to your life?*

   ____

   ____

   ____

   ____

   ____

2. *When was the last time you were given feedback that held you accountable for your actions or behavior?*

   ____

   ____

   ____

   ____

3. *List 2 ways you can become a better friend.*

Black women have been taught to put the needs of their families before their own. The costs associated with this phenomenon is internally damaging because it leads to mental and emotional anguish.

CHAPTER TEN

She's Serious About Self-Care

Self-care is being discussed more frequently because the unexpected twists and turns of 2020 have added a higher level of urgency in efforts to focus on the topic. Before, most people assumed that self-care centered around the notion of being selfish. However, men and women are realizing the need to incorporate self-care into their personal and professional lives more than ever.

It is impossible to effectively pour into others if your cup is empty. You can either choose to make your self-care a priority or life will force you to do it. I had to learn the hard way. After my lovely sister, Alicia, passed, I was forced to make my self-care a priority. My energy levels were drastically different. I went from being high-energy to feeling tired and drained easily. I went from having a predominantly calm, easy-going demeanor to having unexpected anxiety attacks in CrossFit class due to being positioned too close to others on the rowing machines. I went from being the go-to person for the majority of my friends and family to intentionally creating space to focus on me so that I wouldn't feel too overwhelmed.

After experiencing the loss of my sister, I became aware of my limits. I no longer place unrealistic expectations on myself pertaining to my roles in community organizations or with family and friends. I no longer take ownership for the shortcomings of others. Practicing self-care taught me to focus my attention on what really mattered and differentiate my issues from those of the people around me.

One of my company's recent initiatives has been to help others, especially black women, realize that self-care is a necessity, not an option. As a result, we launched a T-shirt initiative called the MY Mental Health = Self Care movement to make mental health a priority, which has received tremendous support from those in the community. Individuals have been encouraged to focus on their mental health and view it as a form of practicing self-care.

There was once a time in which participation in therapy was considered to be a service for "crazy people." However, times have changed. I have discovered that people who participate in therapy tend to be more intentional and effective in other areas of their lives. Therapy is a great tool to help you focus on your self-care. I often tell my clients to make the most of our time together because they will never get an hour of time that is completely focused on them outside of our therapy sessions. I'm biased, but I believe everyone should have a therapist.

Focusing on your mental health is just as important as your physical health. Every aspect of your life: your physical health, intellectual functioning, spirituality, and social functioning, is connected to your emotional well-being. If your mental health is off-balance, everything else in your life will be, too.

There are some practical ways that you can focus on self-care. Most people don't realize that setting boundaries is a form of self-care. Highly productive people practice self-care by being intentional about the boundaries they set in their personal and professional lives. Doing this helps you become more efficient and results in a better version of you.

It is challenging for professional black women, or black women as a whole, to set boundaries because we're accustomed to intermingling multiple tasks that prevent us from pausing to reflect on whether or not we are mentally and emotionally okay. Boundaries will help you and others around you remember what you value. Your boundaries will remind others of how you would like to be treated.

I have come across many single professional black women with no children who have to consistently work at setting boundaries with their families. It is common for families to assume that the single person has time to run errands and take care of everyone else's needs besides her own. In turn, she has a difficult time saying "no" and feels guilty when she does. Her family places troubling responsibilities on her because she allows it. It's okay to say "no."

In another example, a black woman with children and a husband spends so much energy catering to their needs that she neglects her own. It is possible to take care of yourself while you're exerting energy taking care of others. You're just as important, so you must also tend to your needs. As a matter of fact, if you're not taking care of yourself, you're not even able to fully care for those around you like you want to. In Western culture, black women have been taught to put the needs of their families before their own. The costs associated with this phenomenon is internally damaging because it leads to mental and emotional anguish.

Personally, I knew I never wanted to be considered a selfish person. I always had a desire to give and help others mainly because I had been exposed to a lot of selfishness growing up. Because of this, I naturally gave a lot of my time, talents, and energy to others. As a result, I often felt depleted and taken advantage of because I considered others without thinking about my own needs. If you don't set boundaries, you may end up resenting the people around you. I had to learn that people only do what you allow them to, so I became proactive and established boundaries.

If you allow other people to constantly withdraw from you without making deposits into your life, you will end up empty. You have to learn how to make yourself a priority. This will require you to set boundaries and dedicate specific time slots in your schedule to focus on **you**. As a professional black woman pursuing Greatness, you have to get serious about your self-care. If you don't, no one around you will.

CHAPTER 10:

She's Serious About Self-Care

Practical Application - Your Path to Greatness

1. *As a woman of color, what are your thoughts about participating in therapy?*

____

____

____

____

____

2. *List 2 ways you will commit to intentionally focusing on your self-care (include specific activities and how often you will participate).*

____

____

____

____

3. *Write down 2 specific boundaries you would like to establish and with whom.*

EPILOGUE

Now that you have completed *She's a 10: The Black Woman's Guide to Embracing Personal & Professional Greatness*, you are prepared to view obstacles that you encounter personally and professionally as opportunities for growth. You are also equipped to apply practical tools and strategies throughout your journey in life. Additionally, you are ready to embrace exactly what makes you great with boldness. From this day forward, your life will never be the same. Your approach to life will be different. You will now view your personal and professional experiences in life with a solution-oriented, self-enhanced approach. People will no longer be able to put you in a box and limit your capabilities.

I know you may be questioning if you're really prepared to fully embrace the level of Greatness that you have always desired. You are! Now is the time to own what makes you, **you**. Once you do so, the people around you will do the same. You will experience better clarity and gain a greater level of confidence when you realize that you really can experience greatness personally and professionally.

In summary, in Chapter 1, "She's Aware of Her Trauma," you gained insight regarding some of the trauma you may have experienced in childhood, adulthood, and the workplace, as well as how it impacts your thinking. In Chapter 2, "She Tosses Her Superwoman Cape," you learned that it is unrealistic and detrimental to try to be everything to everyone around you. In Chapter 3, "She Walks by Faith," you learned the importance of knowing that everything you experience in life will work out for your good. In Chapter 4, "She Gives Herself Grace for Improvement," you learned that perfectionism is the greatest stumbling block to growth. In Chapter 5, "She's Intentional by Any Means Necessary," you learned the value of being deliberate in every area of your life. In Chapter 6, "She Overcomes Fear," you learned that fear's goal is to keep you trapped in the "what ifs" of the future. In Chapter 7, "She Thinks BIG," you were encouraged to be stretched in your thinking about present and future goals. In Chapter 8, "She Realizes It's Okay Not to be Okay," you were encouraged to embrace your humanity and realize that there will be moments in life when you will not be okay. In Chapter 9, "She Has a Solid Support System," you were encouraged to build quality relationships with people you can trust. In

Chapter 10, "She's Serious About Self-Care," you were informed of the importance of taking care of your needs in the midst of being there for others.

Remember, you are of the utmost importance as you journey through life. If you overcame before, you have the ability to overcome again. Your time is now. Boldly embrace your uniqueness because the next level awaits you. You have nothing to lose but everything to gain.

MY NEXT STEPS FOR PERSONAL GREATNESS

MY NEXT STEPS FOR PROFESSIONAL GREATNESS

www.ingramcontent.com/pod-product-compliance
Lightning Source LLC
LaVergne TN
LVHW051013080826
845145LV00009B/2592